Quick 30-Minute Suppers

Campbell's

EASY SUMMER RECIPES

Preparation and Cooking Times:

Every recipe was developed and tested in the Campbell Kitchens by professional home economists. Use "Chill Time," "Cook Time," "Marinating Time" and/or "Prep Time" given with each recipe as guides. The preparation times are based on the approximate amount of time required to assemble the recipes *before* baking or cooking. These times include preparation steps, such as chopping; mixing; cooking rice, pasta, vegetables; etc. The fact that some preparation steps can be done simultaneously or during cooking is taken into account. The cook times are based on the minimum amount of time required to cook, bake or broil the food in the recipes.

For sending us glassware, flatware, dinnerware and serving pieces used in recipe photographs, a special thanks to: *The Denby Pottery Company,* New York, NY on pages 4, 5 and 23; *Fitz and Floyd,* Dallas, TX on pages 9, 57, 59, 67, 70, 71, 80 and 81; *Lenox China and Crystal,* Lawrenceville, NJ on pages 19, 21, 33 and 39; *Libbey Glass,* Toledo, OH on pages 4, 5 and 91; *Mikasa,* Secaucus, NJ on pages 14, 15, 27, 65, 69, 83 and 89; *Oneida Silversmiths,* Oneida, NY on pages 17, 19, 23, 39, 70 and 71; *The Pfaltzgraff Co.,* York, PA on pages 25, 29, 35, 53, 63, 73, 75, 77, 79 and 89.

Campbell's Easy Summer Recipes was produced by the Publishing Division of Campbell Soup Company, Campbell Place, Camden, NJ 08103-1799.

Corporate Editor:	Pat Teberg
Assistant Editors:	Ginny Gance
	Margaret Romano
Senior Marketing Manager:	Brent Walker
Senior Marketing Research Manager:	Trish Rainone
Campbell Kitchens:	Jane Freiman
Photography:	Peter Walters Photography/Chicago
Photographers:	Peter Walters
	Peter Ross
Photo Stylist/Production:	Betty Karslake
Food Stylists:	Lois Hlavac
	Lee Mooney
	Carol Parik

Designed and published by Meredith Publishing Services, 1912 Grand Avenue, Des Moines, IA 50309-3379. Manufactured in U.S.A.

Pictured on the front cover: Sassy Grilled Chicken *(page 52).*

Campbell's
EASY
SUMMER RECIPES

SHORTCUT SNACKS   4
Sweet and savory snacks for quick nibbling and
easy entertaining—

30-MINUTE SKILLET SUPPERS   14
Quick main-dish recipes to get you in and out of
the kitchen *fast*—

FIRE UP THE GRILL   48
A sizzling selection of savory poultry,
fish, beef and pork entrées—

BUMPER CROP VEGETABLES   70
Fresh from the garden favorites to
serve a few or a hungry crowd—

COOL-AS-A-CUCUMBER SALADS   80
No-fuss main-dish and side-dish pasta
and vegetable salads—

HANDY HERB GUIDE   92
A list of common cooking herbs to
enhance all your summer meals—

INDEX   94

SHORTCUT SNACKS

Hungry and hurried? Nibble on these easy beat-the-heat treats when friends stop by or you need a light snack to curb your appetite. Here's a sampling: lip-smackin'-good *Honey-Mustard Wings*, south-of-the-border *Vegetable Quesadillas*, keep-cool *Quick Gazpacho* and portable *Tomato Soup-Spice Cupcakes.*

Honey-Mustard Wings and Vegetable Quesadillas (pages 6-7).

▼**G**etting the very best out of chicken means following these common sense tips for safe handling.

• Follow directions for cooking chicken thoroughly; heat destroys bacteria.

• Don't place cooked chicken on a platter that has held raw meat.

▼**D**on't let your barbecue grill get the best of **you** when cooking chicken and other meats! To prevent flare-ups, keep the grill clean and trim excess fat from the food before cooking. Remember, even a light breeze across fat-splashed coals can fan flames and result in charred food. If a fire does occur, remove the food and spritz the coals with a spray bottle of water.

HONEY-MUSTARD WINGS

1 pouch CAMPBELL'S Dry Onion with Chicken Broth Soup and Recipe Mix
⅓ cup honey
2 tablespoons spicy brown mustard
18 chicken wings (about 3 pounds)
1 tablespoon vegetable oil

• In small bowl, combine soup mix, honey and mustard; set aside.

• Cut tips off wings; discard tips or save for another use. Cut wings in half at joints to make 36 pieces. In large bowl, place oil and wings; toss to coat.

• To grill: On grill rack, arrange wings directly above medium coals. Grill, uncovered, 30 minutes or until wings are no longer pink, turning once and brushing often with soup mixture during last 10 minutes of cooking time. If desired, garnish with *red onion* and *celery leaves*.

Makes 36 appetizers   **Prep Time: 15 minutes**
Cook Time: 30 minutes

To bake: Prepare sauce and wings as directed above, *except* omit oil. In large bowl, toss wings with soup mixture. In large shallow baking pan, arrange wings. Bake at 400°F. for 25 minutes. Turn wings. Bake 20 minutes more or until wings are no longer pink.

VEGETABLE QUESADILLAS

1 can (10¾ ounces) CAMPBELL'S condensed Cheddar Cheese Soup
¼ cup milk
1 medium tomato, chopped (about 1 cup)
1 medium green pepper, chopped (about ¾ cup)
2 green onions, sliced (about ¼ cup)
1 fresh *or* canned jalapeño pepper, seeded and finely
    chopped (about 1 tablespoon), optional
6 flour tortillas (6 inches *each*)
  Sour cream
  Salsa

• In medium bowl, combine soup, milk, tomato, green pepper, onions and jalapeño pepper.

• On two large baking sheets, arrange tortillas. Top each tortilla with about ⅓ cup soup mixture, spreading evenly to within ½ inch of edge.

• Bake at 400°F. for 10 minutes or until hot and tortillas are crisp. Serve with sour cream and salsa. If desired, garnish with *green onion* and *fresh hot chili pepper*.

Makes 6 quesadillas or 6 appetizer servings	**Prep Time: 15 minutes** **Cook Time: 10 minutes**

▼**W**ear rubber gloves to protect your hands from the burning oils when handling and seeding jalapeño peppers.

▼**T**o protect your tomatoes from losing their flavor, use the sill, not the chill! Never store tomatoes in the refrigerator. Keep them unwashed at room temperature, with the stem end down, on a countertop or windowsill. Chill no more than an hour in the refrigerator before serving.

▼**R**emember, the term "vine-ripened" means that a tomato was harvested when it was turning pink, so rely on yourself to complete what nature started.

To seed a cucumber, cut it in half lengthwise and scoop out the seeds with a teaspoon.

It's easy to add even more zip to this dip! Substitute 1 cup plain yogurt and 1 cup sour cream for the container of sour cream.

Choose from asparagus, sweet peppers, zucchini or yellow squash, green beans, green onions, carrots, celery, cucumbers, snow peas or cherry tomatoes for "dippers." Allow about 4 to 6 vegetable dippers per serving.

Quick Gazpacho

1 can (10¾ ounces) CAMPBELL'S condensed Tomato Soup
1 cup water
2 tablespoons red wine vinegar
1 tablespoon olive oil
1 teaspoon onion powder
⅛ teaspoon garlic powder
1 medium cucumber, seeded and chopped (about 1 cup)
1 small green pepper, chopped (about ½ cup)

• In medium bowl, combine soup, water, vinegar, oil, onion powder and garlic powder. Stir in cucumber and pepper. Cover; refrigerate 2 hours before serving.

Makes about 3 cups or 4 servings

Prep Time: 10 minutes
Chill Time: 2 hours

Broccoli-Onion Dip

1 pouch CAMPBELL'S Dry Onion Soup and Recipe Mix
1 container (16 ounces) sour cream
1 package (10 ounces) frozen chopped broccoli, cooked and drained
Assorted fresh vegetables *or* chips

• In medium bowl, combine soup mix and sour cream. Add broccoli. Cover; refrigerate 2 hours before serving. Serve with fresh vegetables or chips for dipping.

Makes about 3 cups

Prep Time: 10 minutes
Chill Time: 2 hours

Quick Gazpacho *(top)*
Broccoli-Onion Dip *(bottom)*

Nacho Dip

1 can (11 ounces) CAMPBELL'S condensed Fiesta Nacho Cheese Soup
½ cup PACE Salsa
1 bag (about 10 ounces) tortilla chips

• In 1½-quart saucepan, combine soup and salsa. Over low heat, heat through, stirring often. Serve as a dip with tortilla chips. If desired, garnish with *Vlasic sliced pitted ripe olives*, *tomato* and *green onions*

Makes about 1½ cups
or 6 servings

Prep Time: 10 minutes
Cook Time: 5 minutes

Onion Chicken Nuggets

1 pouch CAMPBELL'S Dry Onion with Chicken Broth Soup
and Recipe Mix
⅔ cup dry bread crumbs
⅛ teaspoon pepper
1 egg *or* 2 egg whites
2 tablespoons water
1½ pounds skinless, boneless chicken, cut into 1-inch pieces
2 tablespoons margarine *or* butter, melted (optional)

• With rolling pin, crush soup mix in pouch. On waxed paper, combine soup mix, bread crumbs and pepper.

• In shallow dish, beat together egg and water. Dip chicken into egg mixture; coat with crumb mixture.

• On baking sheet, arrange chicken. Drizzle with margarine. Bake at 400°F. for 15 minutes or until chicken is no longer pink. If desired, garnish with *orange wedges* and *celery leaves*.

Makes 10 appetizer
servings

Prep Time: 20 minutes
Cook Time: 15 minutes

Nacho Dip (top)
Onion Chicken Nuggets (bottom)

It's a snap to soften cream cheese in the microwave. Remove packaging, place on microwave-safe dish and microwave 8 ounces at 50% power (medium) for 1 to 1½ minutes.

TOMATO SOUP-SPICE CUPCAKES

- **2 cups all-purpose flour**
- **1⅓ cups sugar**
- **4 teaspoons baking powder**
- **1½ teaspoons ground allspice**
- **1 teaspoon baking soda**
- **1 teaspoon ground cinnamon**
- **½ teaspoon ground cloves**
- **1 can (10¾ ounces) CAMPBELL'S condensed Tomato Soup**
- **½ cup vegetable shortening**
- **2 eggs**
- **¼ cup water**
- **Cream Cheese Frosting (recipe below)**

• Preheat oven to 350°F. Place paper or foil liners in twenty-four 3-inch muffin cups.

• In mixer bowl, combine first 7 ingredients. Add soup, shortening, eggs and water. Beat at low speed until well mixed, constantly scraping bowl. At high speed, beat 4 minutes, scraping bowl often. Spoon batter into cups, filling each one-half full. Bake 30 minutes. Remove from pans; cool. Frost.

Makes 24 cupcakes   **Prep Time: 20 minutes**
Bake & Cool Time: 1½ hours

CREAM CHEESE FROSTING

- **1 package (8 ounces) cream cheese, softened**
- **2 tablespoons milk**
- **1 teaspoon vanilla extract**
- **1 package (16 ounces) confectioners' sugar (about 4 cups)**

• In bowl with mixer at medium speed, beat cream cheese, milk and vanilla until fluffy. Beat in sugar until smooth. If necessary, add additional milk, 1 teaspoon at a time, until spreading consistency. Makes about 3 cups.

30-MINUTE SKILLET SUPPERS

When time is short, try these speedy skillet suppers. You won't have time to heat up your kitchen—these range-top recipes are ready to enjoy in 30 minutes or less! Try spicy *Nacho Tacos, Lemony Chicken Pasta Toss, Garlic Shrimp and Pasta* and *Easy Beef and Broccoli,* to name a few. Now you'll have time to enjoy yourself this summer!

Nacho Tacos (page 16).

▼ Cilantro, also known as coriander, is a leafy herb from the parsley family that owes its popularity to our growing appetite for Mexican and Oriental foods. For a pleasantly assertive herbal accent, substitute cilantro for parsley in Harvest Chicken Skillet.

▼ How do you take your taco? Toppers like sliced ripe olives, shredded cheese, chopped hot peppers, chopped onions, guacamole and sour cream add color, texture and taste to this traditional Mexican sandwich.

▼ While cooking the meat mixture, heat the taco shells.

HARVEST CHICKEN SKILLET

  2 tablespoons vegetable oil
  4 skinless, boneless chicken breast halves
  1 can (10¾ ounces) CAMPBELL'S condensed Golden Corn Soup
¼ cup milk
¾ teaspoon garlic powder
⅛ teaspoon pepper
1½ cups chopped tomato
  1 tablespoon chopped fresh parsley
  4 cups hot cooked rice

• In skillet over medium-high heat, in hot oil, cook chicken 10 minutes or until browned on both sides. Remove. Pour off fat.

• In skillet, heat soup, milk, garlic and pepper to boiling. Add chicken. Cover; cook over low heat 5 minutes or until chicken is no longer pink, stirring often. Stir in tomato and parsley. Heat. Serve with rice. Garnish with *fresh parsley.*

Makes 4 servings
      Prep Time: 10 minutes
      Cook Time: 20 minutes

NACHO TACOS

  1 pound ground beef
  1 medium onion, chopped (about ½ cup)
½ teaspoon chili powder
  1 can (11 ounces) CAMPBELL'S condensed Fiesta Nacho Cheese Soup
  8 taco shells
  1 cup shredded lettuce
  1 medium tomato, chopped (about 1 cup)

• In skillet over medium-high heat, cook and stir beef, onion and chili powder until beef is browned. Spoon off fat. Add ½ *cup* soup. Reduce heat to low. Heat through, stirring often.

• Heat remaining soup. Divide meat mixture between taco shells. Top with hot soup, lettuce and tomato. Garnish with *tomatoe*s and *fresh cilantro.*

Makes 8 tacos or 4 servings
      Prep Time: 10 minutes
      Cook Time: 10 minutes

LEMONY CHICKEN PASTA TOSS

2 tablespoons cornstarch
1 can (14½ ounces) SWANSON Ready To Serve Clear Chicken Broth
2 tablespoons lemon juice
1 tablespoon Dijon-style mustard
½ teaspoon garlic powder
1 tablespoon olive *or* vegetable oil
1 pound skinless, boneless chicken breasts, cut into strips
3 tablespoons chopped fresh parsley *or* 1 tablespoon
    dried parsley flakes
4 cups hot cooked thin spaghetti (about 8 ounces dry)

• In small bowl, stir together cornstarch, broth, lemon juice, mustard and garlic powder until smooth; set aside.

• In 10-inch skillet over medium-high heat, in hot oil, cook *half* of chicken until browned, stirring often. Remove; set aside. Repeat with remaining chicken. Pour off fat.

• Reduce heat to medium. In same skillet, add reserved cornstarch mixture. Cook until mixture boils and thickens, stirring constantly. Return chicken to skillet. Heat through, stirring occasionally. Stir in parsley. Toss with spaghetti. If desired, garnish with *fresh parsley* and *lemon*.

Makes about 5½ cups   **Prep Time: 10 minutes**
or 4 servings   **Cook Time: 20 minutes**

BUSY-DAY CHICKEN DINNER
Herbed Brown Rice and Chicken
Sliced garden tomatoes and sweet onions with vinaigrette
Sesame bread sticks
Honeydew melon wedges and vanilla ice cream

HERBED BROWN RICE AND CHICKEN

¼ **teaspoon garlic powder**
⅛ **teaspoon pepper**
4 **skinless, boneless chicken breast halves (about 1 pound)**
1 **tablespoon margarine *or* butter**
1 **can (14½ ounces) SWANSON NATURAL GOODNESS Ready To Serve Clear Chicken Broth**
1 **cup frozen peas**
½ **teaspoon dried thyme leaves, crushed**
1½ **cups uncooked quick-cooking brown rice**
2 **tablespoons grated Parmesan cheese**

• On waxed paper, combine garlic powder and pepper; sprinkle over both sides of chicken.

• In 10-inch skillet over medium-high heat, in hot margarine, cook chicken 10 minutes or until browned on both sides. Remove; set aside.

• In same skillet, combine broth, peas and thyme. Heat to boiling. Stir in rice. Return chicken to skillet. Reduce heat to low. Cover; cook 10 minutes or until rice is tender and liquid is absorbed, stirring occasionally. Remove chicken to platter. Stir cheese into rice mixture before serving. If desired, garnish with *fresh thyme, fresh parsley* and *carrots.*

Makes 4 servings   **Prep Time: 5 minutes**
Cook Time: 25 minutes

▼When shopping for skinless, boneless chicken breasts, the chicken meat should be light in color, not gray or pasty looking. Look for a "sell by" label on the package. Most chicken processors specify the last day poultry should be sold. Avoid packages with expired dates.

SHORT-ORDER
SKILLET SUPPER
Chicken in Savory
Lemon Sauce
Mixed green salad with
choice of dressing
Sugar snap peas
Whole wheat rolls
Fresh berries
with vanilla-flavored
yogurt

CHICKEN IN SAVORY LEMON SAUCE

Vegetable cooking spray
4 **skinless, boneless chicken breast halves (about 1 pound)**
1 **can (10¾ ounces) CAMPBELL'S HEALTHY REQUEST condensed**
   Cream of Broccoli Soup
½ **cup water**
¼ **cup chopped sweet red** *or* **green pepper**
1 **tablespoon chopped fresh parsley** *or* **1 teaspoon**
   dried parsley flakes
1 **tablespoon lemon juice**
½ **teaspoon paprika**

• Spray 10-inch nonstick skillet with cooking spray. Heat over medium-high heat 1 minute. Add chicken; cook 10 minutes or until browned on both sides. Remove; set aside.

• In same skillet, combine soup, water, pepper, parsley, lemon juice and paprika. Heat to boiling. Return chicken to skillet. Reduce heat to low. Cover; cook 5 minutes or until chicken is no longer pink, stirring occasionally. If desired, garnish with *fresh parsley* and *lemon*.

Makes 4 servings   **Prep Time: 10 minutes**
                              Cook Time: 20 minutes

It's easy to turn this savory summer sauté into a gourmet classic. Just add ¼ pound medium shrimp, shelled and deveined, to the chicken during the last 5 minutes of cooking. Cook until shrimp turn pink. Next time there's a sale on shrimp, surprise your family with the delightful deep-sea version of this recipe.

EASY-ON-YOU
GRADUATION
CELEBRATION
Sautéed Chicken Breasts
Pasta with
Parmesan cheese
Steamed broccoli and
cauliflower
Fresh strawberry-
rhubarb pie

SAUTÉED CHICKEN BREASTS

2 tablespoons all-purpose flour
⅛ teaspoon pepper
4 skinless, boneless chicken breast halves (about 1 pound)
2 tablespoons vegetable oil
1 can (11⅛ ounces) CAMPBELL'S condensed Italian Tomato Soup
½ cup water

• On waxed paper, combine flour and pepper. Coat chicken lightly with flour mixture.

• In 10-inch skillet over medium-high heat, in hot oil, cook chicken 10 minutes or until browned on both sides. Remove; set aside. Pour off fat.

• In same skillet, combine soup and water. Heat to boiling. Return chicken to skillet. Reduce heat to low. Cover; cook 5 minutes or until chicken is no longer pink, stirring occasionally. If desired, garnish with *fresh rosemary* and *tomato*.

Makes 4 servings

Prep Time: 5 minutes
Cook Time: 20 minutes

▼Celery is a plant from the carrot family, and is also related to parsnips and parsley. When buying celery, select a tightly formed bunch with rigid, crisp "ribs" topped with fresh, hearty-looking leaves. If ribs are rubbery or limp, they're past their prime. Rinse celery in cold water, shake dry and refrigerate in a plastic bag for up to two weeks.

**EASY
30-MINUTE SUPPER**
Herbed Turkey Sauté
Steamed broccoli spears
Cherry tomatoes and
cucumbers with
vinaigrette
Sourdough French bread
Lemon Italian ice

HERBED TURKEY SAUTÉ

2 tablespoons vegetable oil
1 pound turkey breast cutlets *or* slices, cut into strips
2 ribs celery, sliced (about 1 cup)
1 medium onion, chopped (about ½ cup)
½ teaspoon dried thyme leaves, crushed
1 can (10¾ ounces) CAMPBELL'S condensed Cream of Celery Soup
¼ cup water
4 cups hot cooked rice

• In 10-inch skillet over medium-high heat, in *1 tablespoon* hot oil, cook *half* of turkey until browned, stirring often. Remove; set aside. Repeat with remaining turkey.

• Reduce heat to medium. In same skillet, in remaining *1 tablespoon* hot oil, cook celery, onion and thyme until tender, stirring often.

• Stir in soup and water. Heat to boiling. Return turkey to skillet. Heat through, stirring occasionally. Serve over rice. If desired, sprinkle with *paprika;* garnish with *celery leaves* and *tomato.*

Makes 4 servings   **Prep Time: 10 minutes**
                           Cook Time: 20 minutes

Herbed Turkey Sauté

▼To quick-thaw most kinds of frozen vegetables, place in microwave-safe bowl. Cover with vented plastic wrap; microwave on HIGH power for 2 minutes or until thawed.

▼Stir-frys are ideal for speedy summer meals. Start preparing ramen noodle soup according to package directions before you begin cooking the chicken.

CHICKEN AND VEGETABLES

1 can (19 ounces) CAMPBELL'S CHUNKY Ready To Serve
    Chicken Vegetable Soup
½ cup desired frozen vegetables
¼ teaspoon dried oregano leaves, crushed
⅔ cup uncooked quick-cooking rice

• In saucepan over medium heat, heat soup, vegetables and oregano to boiling, stirring often.

• Add rice. Reduce heat to low. Cover; cook 5 minutes or until rice is tender, stirring often. Garnish with *carrot* and *fresh oregano*.

Makes about 3 cups or 2 servings	**Prep Time: 5 minutes** **Cook Time: 10 minutes**

CHUNKY CHICKEN STIR-FRY

1 pound skinless, boneless chicken breasts, cut into strips
1 tablespoon vegetable oil
2 teaspoons cornstarch
1 can (19 ounces) CAMPBELL'S CHUNKY Ready To Serve
    Vegetable Soup
2 teaspoons soy sauce
1 cup frozen vegetable combination, thawed
2 packages (3 ounces *each*) CAMPBELL'S *or* SANWA RAMEN PRIDE
    Chicken Flavor Ramen Noodle Soup, cooked and drained

• In skillet over medium-high heat, stir-fry *half* of chicken in hot oil until browned. Remove; set aside. Repeat with remaining. Pour off fat.

• In same skillet, stir together cornstarch, vegetable soup and soy sauce until cornstarch is dissolved. Add vegetables. Cook and stir until mixture boils and thickens. Return chicken to skillet. Heat through. Serve over noodles.

Makes 4 servings	**Prep Time: 10 minutes** **Cook Time: 15 minutes**

Chicken and Vegetables (top)
Chunky Chicken Stir-Fry (bottom)

In salads, sauces, stuffings, side dishes and entrées, the mushroom has earned its reputation as the world's most respected fungus!

Selecting the freshest mushrooms is a beauty contest, so choose only the most attractive. The caps should be firm, bright and bruise-free. The gills underneath the cap should be tightly closed.

Only wipe mushrooms with a damp cloth or brush lightly with a soft mushroom brush before using -- never soak in water

Use a large pot and plenty of water when cooking pasta. At least 1 quart of water should be used for every 4 ounces of dry pasta. Cook according to package directions, stirring occasionally to keep pieces separate.

PASTA ALFREDO

1 cup sliced fresh mushrooms
2 tablespoons margarine *or* butter
½ cup cooked ham cut in strips
1 can (19 ounces) CAMPBELL'S HOME COOKIN' Ready To Serve Cream of Chicken Soup
1 cup frozen peas
½ cup grated Parmesan cheese
3 cups cooked spaghetti (about 6 ounces dry)

• In 4-quart saucepan over medium heat, cook mushrooms in hot margarine until tender, ham is browned and liquid is evaporated, stirring often.

• Add remaining ingredients. Heat through, stirring often. Garnish with *fresh tarragon.*

Makes about 4 cups or 4 servings

Prep Time: 10 minutes
Cook Time: 10 minutes

CHICKEN PASTA PARMESAN

1 can (19 ounces) CAMPBELL'S HOME COOKIN' Ready To Serve Cream of Mushroom Soup
½ cup grated Parmesan cheese
2 cups cubed cooked chicken *or* turkey
2 tablespoons chopped fresh parsley
4 cups hot cooked thin spaghetti (about 8 ounces dry)

• In 2-quart saucepan, combine soup and cheese. Over medium heat, heat to boiling, stirring often.

• Add chicken and parsley. Heat through, stirring often. Serve over spaghetti. Garnish with *pear slices* and *fresh parsley.*

Makes 4 servings

Prep Time: 10 minutes
Cook Time: 10 minutes

Pasta Alfredo *(top)*
Chicken Pasta Parmesan *(bottom)*

use your nose when selecting fresh fish. Fresh fish has a mild smell, not a "fishy" or ammonia smell. Make sure the flesh feels springy and elastic and appears moist and glistening. The eyes of a whole fish should be clear, never cloudy, dull or sunken. When choosing frozen fillets, make sure the fish is solid, but beware of freezer burn -- sure signs of thawing and refreezing.

**FRIDAY NIGHT FISH
DINNER
Fish and Vegetable
Skillet
New potatoes with
parslied butter
Mixed green salad with
choice of dressing
Medley of sliced fresh
peaches and berries**

FISH AND VEGETABLE SKILLET

2 ribs celery, cut into matchstick-thin strips (about 1 cup)
1 large carrot, cut into matchstick-thin strips (about 1 cup)
1 small onion, diced (about ¼ cup)
¼ cup water
2 tablespoons Chablis or other dry white wine
½ teaspoon dried thyme leaves, crushed Generous dash pepper
**1 can (10¾ ounces) CAMPBELL'S HEALTHY REQUEST condensed
Cream of Mushroom Soup**
**1 pound fresh or thawed frozen firm white fish fillets
(cod, haddock or halibut)**

• In 10-inch skillet, combine celery, carrot, onion, water, wine, thyme and pepper. Over medium-high heat, heat to boiling. Reduce heat to low. Cover; cook 5 minutes or until vegetables are tender-crisp.

• Stir in soup. Over medium heat, heat to boiling. Arrange fish in soup mixture.

• Reduce heat to low. Cover; cook 10 minutes or until fish flakes easily when tested with a fork, spooning sauce over fish occasionally. If desired, garnish with *fresh thyme, bay leaf* and *fluted fresh mushrooms.*

Makes 4 servings   **Prep Time: 10 minutes
Cook Time: 20 minutes**

Fish and Vegetable Skillet

▼Even diehard meat-and-potatoes lovers will be casting their lines for seconds when you serve this delectable poached fish entrée made with flavorful Swanson chicken broth. Substitute 1 pound fresh/frozen firm white fish fillets (cod, haddock or halibut) for the salmon, if you like.

SPECIAL SUNDAY DINNER
Quick 'n' Easy Salmon
Fresh asparagus spears
Orzo with shredded
carrots and basil
Tomato and romaine
salad with Tangy French
Dressing (p. 90)
Melon and blueberries
with lemon frozen
yogurt

QUICK 'N' EASY SALMON

1 can (14½ ounces) SWANSON Ready To Serve
    Clear Chicken Broth
¼ cup Chablis *or* other dry white wine
¼ teaspoon dried dill weed, crushed
4 thin lemon slices
4 salmon steaks, each 1 inch thick (about 1½ pounds)

• In 10-inch skillet, combine broth, wine, dill and lemon. Over medium-high heat, heat to boiling.

• Arrange fish in broth mixture. Reduce heat to low. Cover; cook 10 minutes or until fish flakes easily when tested with a fork. Discard poaching liquid. If desired, serve with *Brussels sprouts*; garnish with *lemon slices, kale leaves* and *fresh dill*.

Makes 4 servings

Prep Time: 10 minutes
Cook Time: 15 minutes

▼**R**eel in family and guests New Orleans-style with this contemporary catch that teams fresh or frozen fish with zesty creole spices and an old family friend -- Campbell's tomato soup. The flavor is big, the preparation is easy!

▼**F**ish fillets cook quickly. You'll need to cook them only 5 minutes in the soup mixture.

FRENCH QUARTER DINNER
Cajun Fish
Green beans with almonds
Shredded carrot and zucchini slaw
Fresh strawberries with shortbread cookies

CAJUN FISH

1 tablespoon vegetable oil
1 small green pepper, diced (about ⅔ cup)
½ teaspoon dried oregano leaves, crushed
1 can (10¾ ounces) **CAMPBELL'S** condensed Tomato Soup
⅓ cup water
⅛ teaspoon garlic powder
⅛ teaspoon black pepper
⅛ teaspoon ground red pepper (cayenne)
4 halibut steaks, each 1 inch thick (about 1½ pounds)
    or 1 pound fresh or thawed frozen firm white
    fish fillets (cod or haddock)
4 cups hot cooked rice

• In 10-inch skillet over medium heat, in hot oil, cook green pepper and oregano until tender, stirring often. Add soup, water, garlic powder, black pepper and red pepper. Heat to boiling, stirring occasionally.

• Arrange fish in soup mixture. Reduce heat to low. Cover; cook 10 minutes or until fish flakes easily when tested with a fork. Serve with rice. If desired, garnish with *fresh parsley* and *fresh chili peppers*.

Makes 4 servings

Prep Time: 10 minutes
Cook Time: 20 minutes

▼It's powerful and irresistible. But deep within it lies a force so intense that spouses, friends and vampires are frequently repelled. It's not the plot of the latest Gothic romance novel, it's garlic! This mystical 5,000-year-old herb certainly has staying power. To remove the odor from your hands after chopping garlic, rub your fingers over a stainless steel spoon under cool running water. A chemical reaction eliminates the smell.

▼You will need to buy at least 1½ pounds raw medium shrimp (in shells) for this recipe.

CASUAL WEEKEND SUPPER
Garlic Shrimp and Pasta
Steamed fresh broccoli and carrots
Crusty French rolls
Cheesecake with fresh raspberries

GARLIC SHRIMP AND PASTA

    2 tablespoons cornstarch
    1 can (14½ ounces) SWANSON Ready To Serve
        Clear Chicken Broth
    3 tablespoons lemon juice
    2 tablespoons olive oil
 1¼ pounds shelled and deveined medium shrimp
    4 cloves garlic, minced
    ⅛ teaspoon ground red pepper (cayenne)
    3 tablespoons chopped fresh parsley or 1 tablespoon
        dried parsley flakes
    5 cups hot cooked extra thin spaghetti (about 8 ounces dry)

• In small bowl, stir together cornstarch, broth and lemon juice until smooth; set aside.

• In 10-inch skillet over medium-high heat, in hot oil, cook shrimp, garlic and red pepper until shrimp turn pink, stirring often. Remove; set aside.

• In same skillet, add reserved cornstarch mixture and parsley. Cook until mixture boils and thickens, stirring constantly. Return shrimp to skillet. Heat through, stirring occasionally. Serve over spaghetti; toss to coat. If desired, garnish with additional *chopped fresh parsley.*

Makes about 6½ cups or 6 servings

Prep Time: 15 minutes
Cook Time: 15 minutes

▼For this "hands-on" recipe, you may substitute 1½ pounds thinly sliced roast turkey for beef. Consider keeping the beef mixture hot in a crockery cooker so your guests can serve themselves at their own pace.

LITTLE LEAGUE TAILGATE
Quick Barbecued Beef
Sandwiches
Onion Bean
Bake (p. 76)
Shortcut Coleslaw
(p. 86)
Tomato Soup-Spice
Cupcakes (p. 12)

QUICK BARBECUED BEEF SANDWICHES

1 tablespoon vegetable oil
1 medium onion, chopped (about ½ cup)
1 can (26 ounces) CAMPBELL'S condensed Tomato Soup
¼ cup water
2 tablespoons packed brown sugar
2 tablespoons vinegar
1 tablespoon Worcestershire sauce
1½ pounds thinly sliced roast beef
12 onion *or* hamburger buns, split and toasted

• In 6-quart Dutch oven over medium heat, in hot oil, cook onion until tender, stirring often.

• Stir in soup, water, brown sugar, vinegar and Worcestershire sauce. Heat to boiling. Reduce heat to low. Cook 5 minutes. Add beef; heat through, stirring occasionally. Serve on buns. If desired, garnish with *Vlasic dill pickle spears, cherry peppers* and *hot peppers.*

Makes about 7 cups or
12 sandwiches

Prep Time: 10 minutes
Cook Time: 20 minutes

▼Kids will love this recipe because it's a sizzling skillet sampler of some of their favorite foods: macaroni, cheese, ground beef and salsa. Don't be surprised if they invite some amigos home to join in one of summer's hottest mealtime hits!

KIDS' SUPPER SPECIAL
Salsa Mac 'n' Beef
Corn bread and
honey butter
Mixed green salad with
choice of dressing
Brownies and
vanilla ice cream

SALSA MAC 'N' BEEF

1 pound ground beef
2 cans (14½ ounces *each*) SWANSON Ready To Serve Clear Beef Broth
3 cups dry medium shell macaroni *or* 2 cups dry elbow macaroni
1 can (10¾ ounces) CAMPBELL'S condensed Cheddar Cheese Soup
½ cup PACE Salsa

• In 10-inch skillet over medium-high heat, cook beef until browned, stirring to separate meat. Spoon off fat.

• Add broth. Heat to boiling. Stir in macaroni. Reduce heat to medium. Cook 10 minutes or until macaroni is tender, stirring often.

• Stir in soup and salsa. Heat through, stirring occasionally. If desired, garnish with *fresh cilantro* and *shredded Cheddar cheese*.

Makes about 6 cups or   **Prep Time: 5 minutes**
4 servings   **Cook Time: 25 minutes**

Easy Beef and Broccoli

2 teaspoons cornstarch
1 can (19 ounces) CAMPBELL'S CHUNKY Ready To Serve
    Old Fashioned Vegetable Beef Soup
1 cup cooked broccoli flowerets
⅛ teaspoon pepper
2 cups hot cooked rice
    Shredded Cheddar cheese

• In saucepan, stir together cornstarch and soup until cornstarch is dissolved. Add broccoli and pepper. Over medium heat, cook until mixture boils, stirring often. Serve over rice. Sprinkle with cheese. Garnish with *red onion* and *celery leaves.*

Makes 2 servings   **Prep Time: 15 minutes**
                             Cook Time: 5 minutes

Skillet Beef Supper

1 pound boneless beef sirloin *or* top round steak, ¾ inch thick
1 tablespoon vegetable oil
1 can (19 ounces) CAMPBELL'S HOME COOKIN' Ready To Serve
    Cream of Mushroom Soup
¼ teaspoon pepper
4 cups hot cooked egg noodles

• Slice beef across the grain into thin strips.

• In skillet over medium-high heat, in hot oil, cook *half* of beef until browned, stirring often. Remove; set aside. Repeat. Pour off fat.

• In same skillet, combine soup and pepper. Heat to boiling. Return beef to skillet. Reduce heat to low. Heat through, stirring occasionally. Serve over noodles. Garnish with *fresh parsley.*

Makes 4 servings   **Prep Time: 10 minutes**
                             Cook Time: 20 minutes

Easy Beef and Broccoli (top)
Skillet Beef Supper (bottom)

One of the best-kept secrets in the produce aisle is that pricey sweet red bell peppers are actually green bell peppers that have been allowed to ripen on the bush. If you find that red peppers are worth the wait and extra cost, dice them and store in the freezer. Add, still frozen, to practically any dish simmering on the range-top.

Ham and Pasta Skillet makes a satisfying summer meal that saves on money and prep time. Instead of buying a shank, rump or whole ham that you're not likely to use up quickly, pick up just the amount of cooked ham you need at your supermarket deli.

SAUSAGE AND PEPPER SANDWICHES

    1 pound bulk pork sausage
    1 small green pepper, chopped (about ½ cup)
    1 can (11⅛ ounces) CAMPBELL'S condensed Italian Tomato Soup
    4 Kaiser rolls, split and toasted

• In 10-inch skillet over medium-high heat, cook sausage and pepper until meat is browned, stirring to separate meat. Spoon off fat.

• Stir in soup. Heat through, stirring often. Serve on rolls. Garnish with *tomatoes* and *celery*.

Makes about 3 cups or	Prep Time: 10 minutes
4 servings	Cook Time: 10 minutes

HAM AND PASTA SKILLET

    1 can (10¾ ounces) CAMPBELL'S condensed Broccoli Cheese Soup
    1 cup milk
    1 tablespoon spicy brown mustard
    2 cups fresh broccoli flowerets
    3 cups cooked medium shell macaroni (about 2 cups dry)
1½ cups cooked ham cut in thin strips

• In 10-inch skillet, combine soup, milk and mustard; add broccoli. Over medium heat, heat to boiling, stirring often. Reduce heat to low. Cover; cook 5 minutes or until broccoli is tender, stirring often.

• Add macaroni and ham. Heat through, stirring often. Garnish with *plum slices* and *fresh mint*.

Makes about 6 cups or	Prep Time: 10 minutes
4 servings	Cook Time: 15 minutes

Sausage and Pepper Sandwiches (top)
Ham and Pasta Skillet (bottom)

FIRE UP THE GRILL

Add summertime sizzle to everyday chicken, fish, beef and pork! And with Campbell's you can create irresistible backyard barbecue feasts all summer long. Choose from *Herbed Chicken Kabobs, Bistro Onion Burgers, Chicken Fajitas* and *Honey-Barbecued Ribs,* for example. So turn the page and fire up the grill for surefire success!

Sassy Grilled Chicken (page 52).

GREAT GRILLING-
BEGIN WITH THE BASICS

Whether you're cooking on the backyard grill, over coals on the beach or on a hibachi at a campsite, take a few minutes to brush up on some surefire barbecue pointers.

Choosing a Grill

Before purchasing a grill, consider where you will be grilling, what you will be cooking and the season for most of your outdoor cooking. If you're typically cooking for a few people, select a smaller grill. For larger crowds, a large covered grill maybe worth the extra expense.

What fuels the fire is a matter of personal choice—gas, electric or charcoal. The advantage of gas and electric grills is their fast starting, quick preheating time and accurate heat control.

Building a Charcoal Fire

Make sure the grill is in a well-ventilated area. Some manufacturers suggest lining the firebox with heavy-duty foil and a bedding of about one inch of small gravel. After using the grill about a dozen times, change the foil and bedding.

Start the briquettes about 30 minutes before you begin cooking. The charcoal will burn evenly and develop an intense heat.

To determine the amount of charcoal necessary, arrange the briquettes in a single layer one inch beyond the size of the food to be grilled. (On humid or windy days, you'll need a few more briquettes.) Then, stack the briquettes in a pyramid-shaped pile in the center of the grill.

Lighting the Fire

Some briquettes are pretreated and can be ignited with a single match. However, most charcoal briquettes need liquid or a jelly fire starter. Just drizzle it over all of the briquettes and wait a minute before lighting. For a faster start, try an electric starter.

Once all of the coals are ash grey by day or glowing red after dark, spread coals in a single layer with long-handled tongs for direct cooking. The coals are arranged around a disposable drip pan for indirect cooking. All of the grill recipes in this book are cooked four inches directly above medium coals.

Judging the Temperature of the Coals

To determine the temperature of the coals, hold the palm of your hand above the coals at the height the food is to be cooked. Count the number of seconds you can hold your hand in that position before the heat forces you to pull it away.

Time	Temperature
2 seconds	hot (high)
3 seconds	medium-hot
4 seconds	medium
5 seconds	medium-slow
6 seconds	slow

Adjusting the Heat

Here are some tips for adjusting the temperature of the coals:

If the coals are too hot: raise the grill rack, spread the coals apart, remove some hot coals or close the air vents on the grill. If using a gas or electric grill, lower the temperature setting.

If the coals are too cool: remove the grill grid and tap the ashes off the coals, move the coals close together, add more coals, lower the grill rack or open the vents. For a gas or electric grill, increase the temperature setting.

Cleaning the Grill

The best time to clean the grill grid is while it is still warm. A stiff metal brush is ideal for scraping off cooked-on food. Don't brush too hard or you may ruin the grid's protective coating. After the grill grid has cooled, soak it in hot sudsy water. If the grid is too large to soak, then cover it with wet, sudsy paper towels and let it stand for about an hour before cleaning.

Grilling Safety Tips

• Always use tools with long handles to protect your arm and hand from the heat of the grill.
• Grill in a well-ventilated area and on a level surface.
• Do not add starter once the briquettes have been lit.
• Watch for flare-ups: Remove the food from the grill and mist the coals. Avoid flare-ups by making sure the heat is even, trimming fat from meat before cooking and cleaning the grill grid often.

▼Nothing beats skewers for keeping small pieces of food from falling into the coals. Metal skewers with a square shape help keep food from moving around when you turn it. If you use bamboo skewers, soak them in warm water for 30 minutes before using on the grill to keep them from burning.

▼Grill vegetables alongside your meat. Use heavy-duty foil to wrap corn on the cob, whole potatoes or a mixture of cut-up fresh vegetables. Seal tightly and grill directly over medium coals until tender, about 40-60 minutes (for corn and potatoes), 20-30 minutes for other vegetables. This not only seals in the natural flavors, but makes the grill a little easier to clean.

HERBED CHICKEN KABOBS

   1 pouch CAMPBELL'S Dry Onion with Chicken Broth Soup and Recipe Mix
   ½ cup water
   2 tablespoons vegetable oil
   ½ teaspoon dried thyme leaves, crushed
   ¼ teaspoon pepper
   ⅛ teaspoon garlic powder
   1 pound skinless, boneless chicken breasts, cut into 1-inch pieces
   1 green pepper, cut into 1-inch squares
   1 sweet red pepper, cut into 1-inch squares

• In glass bowl, combine first 6 ingredients. Add chicken; toss. Cover; chill at least 1 hour.

• Remove chicken; reserve marinade. On four 10-inch skewers, thread chicken and peppers.

• Grill kabobs directly above medium coals, uncovered, 15 minutes or until chicken is no longer pink, turning often and brushing with marinade. Garnish with *lemon* and *fresh chervil*.

Makes 4 servings	**Marinating Time: 1 hour**
Prep Time: 15 minutes	**Cook Time: 15 minutes**

SASSY GRILLED CHICKEN

   1 can (26 ounces) CAMPBELL'S condensed Tomato Soup
   ¼ cup honey
   2 teaspoons dry mustard
   1 teaspoon onion powder
   8 chicken breast halves

• In saucepan, combine first 4 ingredients. Grill chicken directly above medium coals, uncovered, 40 minutes or until chicken is no longer pink, turning often and brushing with sauce.

• Heat remaining sauce to boiling. If desired, serve chicken with *grilled vegetables*.

Makes 8 servings	**Prep Time: 10 minutes**
	Cook Time: 45 minutes

▼Flour tortillas are a versatile Mexican bread. Prevent flour tortillas from drying out in a conventional oven by wrapping them in foil. If you're in a rush, wrap them in damp paper towels and microwave them.

▼Similarly, you may expedite the ripening process for avocados in this recipe. Place them in a slightly closed paper or plastic bag. Store at room temperature for one to three days.

QUICK FIESTA SUPPER
Broccoli-Onion
Dip (p. 8)
Chicken Fajitas
Fresh apple and
spinach salad
Ice cream sundaes

CHICKEN FAJITAS

6 skinless, boneless chicken breast halves (about 1½ pounds)
¼ cup prepared Italian salad dressing
1 can (10¾ ounces) CAMPBELL'S condensed Cheddar Cheese Soup
½ cup PACE Salsa
12 flour tortillas (6 inches *each*)
4 green onions, thinly sliced (about ½ cup)
1 small avocado, peeled, seeded and sliced (optional)

• In large shallow nonmetallic dish, arrange chicken. Pour vinaigrette over chicken, turning to coat. Cover; refrigerate at least 30 minutes.

• To grill: Remove chicken from marinade and arrange on grill rack directly above medium coals; discard marinade. Grill, uncovered, 15 minutes or until chicken is no longer pink, turning once during cooking.

• In 1-quart saucepan, combine soup and salsa. Over medium heat, heat through, stirring occasionally. Meanwhile, heat tortillas according to package directions.

• Slice chicken into thin strips. Arrange down center of each tortilla; top with onions, avocado and soup mixture. Fold or roll tortilla around filling. If desired, garnish with *lemon and lime wedges, fresh cilantro* and *green onion*.

Makes 6 servings	**Marinating Time: 30 minutes**
Prep Time: 5 minutes	**Cook Time: 15 minutes**

**MEMORIAL DAY
COOKOUT**
Honey-Mustard
Wings (p. 6)
Oriental Shrimp Kabobs
Glazed Peas and
Carrots (p. 74)
Noodles with fresh herbs
Mixed green salad with
choice of dressing
Watermelon basket
filled with assorted
fresh fruit

ORIENTAL SHRIMP KABOBS

1 can (10¾ ounces) CAMPBELL'S condensed Tomato Soup
¼ cup orange juice
1 tablespoon soy sauce
1 tablespoon vegetable oil
¼ teaspoon ground ginger
1½ pounds large shrimp, shelled and deveined

• In large shallow nonmetallic dish, combine soup, orange juice, soy sauce, oil and ginger. Add shrimp; toss to coat. Cover; refrigerate at least 1 hour.

• Remove shrimp from marinade; reserve marinade. On six 10-inch skewers, thread shrimp.

• To grill: On grill rack, arrange kabobs directly above medium coals. Grill, uncovered, 10 minutes or until shrimp turn pink, turning often and brushing with marinade during cooking.

• In 1-quart saucepan over medium heat, heat remaining marinade to boiling. Serve with shrimp. If desired, serve on bed of shredded *salad greens*; garnish with *fresh pineapple slices* and *orange peel.*

Makes 6 servings   **Marinating Time: 1 hour**
Prep Time: 20 minutes   **Cook Time: 15 minutes**

To broil: On rack in broiler pan, arrange kabobs. Broil 4 inches from heat 5 minutes or until shrimp turn pink, turning often and brushing with marinade during cooking.

▼Fish Steaks Dijon is equally delicious served chilled.

▼When it comes to grilling fish, one good turn doesn't deserve another! Fish is more delicate than beef, chicken and pork, so avoid over-handling it when it's on the grill. One turn with a thin sharp-edge spatula for each fish steak is plenty.

SUMMER CONCERT TAILGATE
Fish Steaks Dijon
Crunchy Potato Salad (p. 88)
Red and green cabbage vinaigrette
Cheddar bread sticks
Medley of fresh fruit

FISH STEAKS DIJON

1 can (14½ ounces) SWANSON Ready To Serve
   Clear Chicken Broth
3 tablespoons olive oil
2 tablespoons lemon juice
1 tablespoon Dijon-style mustard
⅛ teaspoon pepper
6 swordfish *or* salmon steaks, 1 inch thick (about 2¼ pounds)

• In large shallow nonmetallic dish, with fork or wire whisk, combine broth, oil, lemon juice, mustard and pepper. Add fish, turning to coat. Cover; refrigerate at least 1 hour, turning fish occasionally.

• To grill: Remove fish from marinade and arrange on grill rack directly above medium coals; reserve marinade. Grill, uncovered, 10 minutes or until fish flakes easily when tested with a fork, turning once and brushing often with marinade during cooking. Discard remaining marinade. If desired, garnish with *lemon wedges* and *fresh basil*.

Makes 6 servings	**Marinating Time: 1 hour**
Prep Time: 10 minutes	**Cook Time: 10 minutes**

To broil: On rack in broiler pan, arrange marinated fish. Broil 4 inches from heat 8 minutes or until fish flakes easily when tested with a fork, turning once and brushing often with marinade during cooking. Discard marinade.

BISTRO ONION BURGERS

1 pouch CAMPBELL'S Dry Onion Soup and Recipe Mix
3 tablespoons water
1½ pounds ground beef
6 PEPPERIDGE FARM Hamburger Buns, split and toasted

• In large bowl, combine soup mix and water. Add beef; mix *thoroughly*. Shape meat mixture *firmly* into 6 patties, ½ inch thick.

• To grill: On grill rack, arrange patties directly above medium coals. Grill, uncovered, until desired doneness (allow about 10 minutes for medium, 160°F.), turning once during cooking. If desired, brush with Favorite Barbecue Sauce (p. 66) during cooking. Serve on buns. If desired, serve with *lettuce, tomato,* and *red onion;* garnish with *Vlasic bread and butter pickles* and *carrots.*

Makes 6 servings

Prep Time: 10 minutes
Cook Time: 10 minutes

To broil: On rack in broiler pan, arrange patties. Broil 4 inches from heat until desired doneness (allow 10 minutes for medium, 160°F.), turning once during cooking.

Bistro Onion Burgers

GRILLED MARINATED BEEF

1 can (10¾ ounces) CAMPBELL'S condensed Tomato Soup
¼ cup water
1 tablespoon lemon juice
2 teaspoons Dijon-style mustard
1 teaspoon Worcestershire sauce
1½ pounds boneless beef sirloin steak, 1 inch thick

• In small bowl, combine soup, water, lemon juice, mustard and Worcestershire sauce. Reserve *¾ cup*; refrigerate.

• Pour remaining marinade into large shallow nonmetallic dish. Add steak, turning to coat. Cover; refrigerate at least 2 hours, turning occasionally.

• To grill: Remove steak from marinade and place on grill rack directly above medium coals; discard marinade. Grill, uncovered, until desired doneness (allow 25 minutes for medium), turning once during cooking.

• Meanwhile, in 1-quart saucepan over medium heat, heat reserved soup mixture to boiling. Thinly slice steak, serve with soup mixture. Serve with *sautéed zucchini* and *mashed potatoes*. If desired, sprinkle with *lemon-pepper seasoning;* garnish with *fresh marjoram.*

Makes 6 servings   **Marinating Time: 2 hours**
Prep Time: 10 minutes   **Cook Time: 25 minutes**

To broil: On rack in broiler pan, place marinated steak. Broil 4 inches from heat until desired doneness (allow 20 minutes for medium), turning once during cooking.

Grilled Marinated Beef

FOURTH OF JULY PICNIC
Honey-Barbecued Ribs
Sassy Grilled
Chicken (p. 52)
Corn on the cob
Shortcut Coleslaw
(p. 86)
Buttermilk biscuits
Tomato Soup-Spice
Cupcakes (p. 12)

HONEY-BARBECUED RIBS

4 pounds pork spareribs
1 pouch CAMPBELL'S Dry Onion Soup and Recipe Mix
¾ cup ketchup
¾ cup water
⅓ cup honey
½ teaspoon pepper
¼ teaspoon garlic powder *or* 2 cloves garlic, minced

• Cut ribs into 2- or 3-rib portions. In 6-quart Dutch oven, place ribs; add cold water to cover. Over high heat, heat to boiling. Reduce heat to low. Cover; cook 45 minutes. Drain.

• Meanwhile, in 1-quart saucepan, combine soup mix, ketchup, water, honey, pepper and garlic powder. Over high heat, heat to boiling. Reduce heat to low. Cook 5 minutes, stirring occasionally.

• To grill: On grill rack, arrange ribs directly above medium coals. Grill, uncovered, 30 minutes, turning often and brushing with sauce during cooking. If desired, serve with *orange-onion salad* and *Pepperidge Farm French bread*.

Makes 4 servings   **Prep Time: 10 minutes**
                              Cook Time: 1½ hours

To bake: In large shallow roasting pan, arrange ribs. Pour sauce over ribs, turning to coat. Bake at 400°F. for 20 minutes. Turn ribs; spoon sauce over ribs. Bake 20 minutes more or until glazed.

▼**W**hat do Model Ts and outdoor cooking have in common? The answer is Henry Ford, the father of the charcoal briquet! Instead of discarding scrap wood leftover from the production of automobile frames, the frugal car czar had a better idea. He burned it, ground it and pressed it into the small blocks that revolutionized the truly American pastime of backyard barbecuing.

▼**I**n Japanese, "teri" (shiny/glazed) and "yaki" means a food that has been marinated/glazed with a soy sauce mixture, then grilled.

▼**S**elect long-handled, square-shaped metal skewers for these kabobs. When you turn the skewers, the pieces of pork, onion and mushroom will remain securely in place.

Favorite Barbecue Sauce

　1　can (10¾ ounces) CAMPBELL'S condensed Tomato Soup
　¼　cup vinegar
　¼　cup vegetable oil
　2　tablespoons packed brown sugar
　1　tablespoon Worcestershire sauce
　1　teaspoon garlic powder
　⅛　teaspoon Louisiana-style hot sauce (optional)

• In bowl, combine all ingredients. Use as a grilling sauce for poultry or meat.

Makes 1⅓ cups sauce　　　**Prep Time: 5 minutes**

Teriyaki Pork Kabobs

　2　tablespoons cornstarch
　1　can (14½ ounces) SWANSON Ready To Serve Clear Beef Broth
　2　tablespoons soy sauce
　1　tablespoon packed brown sugar
　¼　teaspoon garlic powder
　¼　teaspoon ground ginger
　1　pound boneless pork loin, cut into 1-inch pieces
12　medium fresh mushrooms
　1　large red onion, cut into 12 wedges
　4　cherry tomatoes

• In saucepan, stir together first 6 ingredients until smooth. Over medium heat, cook until mixture boils, stirring constantly.

• On four 10-inch skewers, thread pork, mushrooms and onion. Grill kabobs directly above medium coals, uncovered, 20 minutes or until pork is no longer pink, turning and brushing with sauce. Place tomatoes on kabobs.

• Heat remaining sauce to boiling. Serve with kabobs and *hot cooked rice*. Garnish with *fresh chives*.

Makes 4 servings　　　**Prep Time: 15 minutes**
　　　　　　　　　　　　　Cook Time: 25 minutes

Favorite Barbecue Sauce (top)
Teriyaki Pork Kabobs (bottom)

▼**B**ranch out! For a smoky flavor, add presoaked hardwood chips like oak, hickory or mesquite to your barbecue coals. Fresh cuttings from any fruitwood tree give a mildly sweet flavor to the food.

▼**L**eave space on skewers between pieces of food to allow the hot air to circulate and help cook the food evenly.

Herb Grilling Sauce

    1 can (14½ ounces) SWANSON Ready To Serve
        Clear Chicken Broth
    3 tablespoons lemon juice
    1 teaspoon dried basil leaves, crushed
    1 teaspoon dried thyme leaves, crushed
    ⅛ teaspoon pepper

• In small bowl, combine broth, lemon juice, basil, thyme and pepper. Use to baste pork, chicken or fish during grilling.

Makes about 2 cups   **Prep Time: 10 minutes**

Potato Kabobs with Cheese Sauce

    6 medium baking potatoes (about 2¼ pounds)
    2 tablespoons vegetable oil
    1 can (10¾ ounces) CAMPBELL'S condensed Cheddar Cheese Soup
    ⅓ cup milk

• Cut potatoes in half lengthwise; cut each half crosswise into 4 pieces.

• On six 10-inch skewers, thread potatoes. Brush potatoes with oil. On grill rack, arrange kabobs directly above medium coals. Grill, uncovered, 30 minutes or until potatoes are fork-tender, turning once during cooking.

• Meanwhile, in 1-quart saucepan, combine soup and milk. Over low heat, heat through, stirring occasionally. Serve over potatoes. If desired, sprinkle with *paprika*.

Makes 6 servings   **Prep Time: 10 minutes**
                        Cook Time: 30 minutes

Herb Grilling Sauce *(left)*
Potato Kabobs with Cheese Sauce *(right)*

BUMPER CROP VEGETABLES

Vegetables ARE versatile! So take advantage of the bounty of the season with these fast-fixing side-dish recipes. From colorful *Pasta Primavera* and zesty *Italian Potato Topper* to *Potluck Vegetable Rotini* and hearty *Onion Bean Bake,* you'll find just the recipe here to satisfy hungry appetites all summer long!

Pasta Primavera
(page 72).

Italian Potato Topper

1 can (10¾ ounces) **CAMPBELL'S** condensed Cream of Mushroom Soup
¼ cup grated Parmesan cheese
   Dash pepper
2 cups frozen Italian-style vegetables
4 hot baked potatoes, split
   Chopped tomato

• In saucepan, combine soup, cheese and pepper. Over medium heat, heat to boiling. Add vegetables. Reduce heat to low. Cover; cook 5 minutes, stirring often. Serve over potatoes. Top with tomato. Garnish with *fresh parsley.*

Makes about 2 cups sauce or 4 side-dish servings	Prep Time: 5 minutes Cook Time: 10 minutes

Pasta Primavera

2 tablespoons cornstarch
1 can (14½ ounces) **SWANSON NATURAL GOODNESS**
   Ready To Serve Clear Chicken Broth
1 teaspoon dried oregano leaves, crushed
¼ teaspoon garlic powder
2 cups fresh broccoli flowerets
2 medium carrots, diagonally sliced
1 medium onion, cut into wedges
1 medium tomato, diced
4 cups hot cooked thin spaghetti (about 8 ounces dry)
   Grated Parmesan cheese

• In cup, stir together cornstarch and *¾ cup* of broth until smooth; set aside.

• In saucepan over medium-high heat, heat remaining broth, oregano and garlic powder to boiling. Add broccoli, carrots and onion. Cover; cook over medium heat 5 minutes.

• Add cornstarch mixture. Cook until mixture boils and thickens, stirring constantly. Stir in tomato. Toss with spaghetti. Serve with cheese.

Makes about 7 cups or 4 side-dish servings	Prep Time: 15 minutes Cook Time: 15 minutes

▼Snow peas are also known as Chinese pea pods. Look for firm, crisp, bright green pods from February to June. To store, place unwashed pods in a plastic bag and refrigerate up to three days. Before cooking, remove strings, break off both ends and rinse in cold water.

▼While many of summer's social scenes are impromptu picnics in a neighbor's backyard, proper food handling is something that should never be left to chance. In hot weather, serve already-prepared foods directly from a cooler. Wrap the casserole dish for hot foods like Potluck Vegetable Rotini in newspaper and dish towels for more insulation.

GLAZED PEAS AND CARROTS

4 teaspoons cornstarch
1 can (16 ounces) CAMPBELL'S HEALTHY REQUEST
  Ready To Serve Chicken Broth
1 teaspoon lemon juice
4 medium carrots, diagonally sliced
1 medium onion, coarsely chopped
2 cups snow peas (about 8 ounces)

• Combine cornstarch, *½ cup* broth and juice.

• In skillet over medium heat, heat remaining broth to boiling. Add carrots and onion. Cover; cook and stir 5 minutes.

• Add peas and cornstarch mixture. Cook until mixture boils, stirring constantly. Garnish with *nasturtium leaves* and *red onion*.

| Makes about 4 cups or | Prep Time: 10 minutes |
| 5 side-dish servings | Cook Time: 15 minutes |

POTLUCK VEGETABLE ROTINI

5 cups dry corkscrew macaroni
2 bags (16 ounces *each*) frozen vegetable combination
1 can (26 ounces) CAMPBELL'S condensed Cream of Chicken Soup
1 package (3 ounces) cream cheese
1 cup milk
½ cup grated Parmesan cheese
⅛ teaspoon pepper

• Cook macaroni, adding vegetables last 5 minutes of cooking time. Drain.

• In Dutch oven, stir soup into cream cheese; add remaining ingredients. Over low heat, heat until cream cheese is melted, stirring often. Add macaroni and vegetables; toss. Heat through. Garnish with *fresh chives*.

| Makes about 14 cups or | Prep Time: 10 minutes |
| 14 side-dish servings | Cook Time: 30 minutes |

Glazed Peas and Carrots *(top)*
Potluck Vegetable Rotini *(bottom)*

ONION BEAN BAKE

2 cans (28 ounces *each*) CAMPBELL'S Pork & Beans in Tomato Sauce
1 pouch CAMPBELL'S Dry Onion Soup and Recipe Mix
2 tablespoons maple-flavored syrup
4 slices bacon, halved and partially cooked

• In 2-quart casserole, combine beans, soup mix and syrup. Arrange bacon on beans. Bake at 350°F. for 1 hour or until hot and bubbling. If desired, garnish with *red onion* and *fresh oregano*.

Makes about 5½ cups or 11 side-dish servings

Prep Time: 10 minutes
Cook Time: 1 hour

TOMATO-BASIL ZUCCHINI

1 can (10¾ ounces) CAMPBELL'S HEALTHY REQUEST condensed Tomato Soup
2 tablespoons grated Parmesan cheese
1 tablespoon lemon juice
½ teaspoon garlic powder
½ teaspoon dried basil leaves, crushed
4 medium zucchini, sliced (about 6 cups)
1 medium green pepper, cut into strips (about 1 cup)
1 large onion, thinly sliced (about 1 cup)

• In 6-quart Dutch oven, combine soup, cheese, lemon juice, garlic powder and basil. Over medium heat, heat to boiling, stirring often.

• Add zucchini, pepper and onion; toss to coat. Reduce heat to low. Cover; cook 15 minutes or until vegetables are tender, stirring often. If desired, garnish with additional *grated Parmesan cheese*.

Makes about 6 cups or 8 side-dish servings

Prep Time: 15 minutes
Cook Time: 20 minutes

Onion Bean Bake *(top)*
Tomato-Basil Zucchini *(bottom)*

MARINATED VEGETABLES

1 can (14½ ounces) SWANSON Ready To Serve Clear Vegetable Broth
1 tablespoon sugar
½ teaspoon dried thyme leaves, crushed
¼ teaspoon garlic powder
⅛ teaspoon pepper
4 cups cauliflowerets (about 1 small head)
1½ cups green beans cut in 1-inch pieces
2 medium carrots, sliced (about 1 cup)
¼ cup vinegar
2 tablespoons chopped fresh parsley

• In saucepan, combine first 5 ingredients; add vegetables. Cover; heat to boiling. Stir. Cook 1 minute. Add vinegar and parsley. Spoon into dish. Cover; chill 12 hours before serving.

Makes about 6 cups or 12 side-dish servings

Prep Time: 15 minutes
Cook Time: 10 minutes
Marinating Time: 12 hours

BASIL VEGETABLE MEDLEY

1 tablespoon vegetable oil
¾ pound fresh asparagus spears (about 12 to 15), trimmed and cut into 1-inch pieces
2 medium carrots, thinly sliced (about ⅔ cup)
¼ teaspoon dried basil leaves, crushed
1 cup sliced fresh mushrooms
1 can (10¾ ounces) CAMPBELL'S condensed Cream of Asparagus Soup
2 tablespoons milk

• In saucepan over medium heat, in hot oil, cook asparagus, carrots and basil until tender-crisp, stirring often. Add mushrooms; cook until tender, stirring often. Stir in soup and milk. Heat through. Garnish with *carrots* and *fresh thyme*.

Makes about 3 cups or 6 side-dish servings

Prep Time: 15 minutes
Cook Time: 15 minutes

Marinated Vegetables *(top)*
Basil Vegetable Medley *(bottom)*

COOL-AS-A-CUCUMBER SALADS

Ahh, summer! Salads are a refreshing way to add color and crunch to any hot-weather meal. Choose from such fresh-tasting main-dish and side-dish favorites as *Grilled Chicken Salad, Tuna Macaroni Salad* and *Crunchy Potato Salad.* Try our simple salad dressings to drizzle over a bowl of mixed garden greens or cut-up fresh fruit!

Grilled Chicken Salad (page 82).

Your family will twist 'n' shout for more of this super salad! Two whole uncooked chicken breasts—1½ pounds with skin and bones, ¾ pound without—yield the 2 cups you'll need to prepare this recipe. Two 5-ounce cans of Swanson premium chunk chicken, drained, also yields 2 cups.

Avoid a sticky situation with your pasta by making sure not to overcook it. After cooking, rinse pasta immediately, then drain again.

How green was my salad? The greener the better! Avoid bunches with thick, coarsely-veined leaves when choosing salad greens. Choose tender leaves free of blemishes and brown, moist residue.

CHICKEN 'N' TWISTS

- 1 can (14½ ounces) SWANSON NATURAL GOODNESS Ready To Serve Clear Chicken Broth
- ½ cup reduced-calorie mayonnaise
- ¼ cup grated Parmesan cheese
- 1 teaspoon dried dill weed
- 3 cups hot cooked corkscrew macaroni
- 2 cups cubed cooked chicken
- 1 cup cherry tomatoes, each cut in half
- 1 cup frozen peas
- ½ cup sliced fresh mushrooms
- 1 small red onion, chopped (about ¼ cup)

• In large bowl, with fork combine first 4 ingredients. Add remaining ingredients; toss to coat. Cover; chill 6 hours, stirring often. Serve on lettuce. Garnish with *fresh dill.*

Makes about 9 cups or 4 main-dish servings

Prep Time: 20 minutes
Chill Time: 6 hours

GRILLED CHICKEN SALAD

- 1 can (10¾ ounces) CAMPBELL'S condensed Tomato Soup
- 1 tablespoon soy sauce
- 1 tablespoon vinegar
- ¼ teaspoon ground ginger
- ⅛ teaspoon garlic powder
- 4 skinless, boneless chicken breast halves
- 8 cups salad greens torn in bite-size pieces

• In saucepan, combine first 5 ingredients.

• Grill chicken directly above medium coals, uncovered, 15 minutes or until chicken is no longer pink, turning once and brushing with sauce. Heat remaining sauce to boiling. Slice chicken into strips. Serve chicken on greens with sauce. Garnish with *lemon peel.*

Makes 4 main-dish servings

Prep Time: 15 minutes
Cook Time: 15 minutes

▼**H**ere's a hot tip: Chili powder comes from the combination of dried chilies, cumin, coriander, cloves, oregano and garlic. Use hot chili powder for a spicier salad. If you like, pass your favorite salsa to spoon over.

EASY SUMMER SUPPER
Chicken Taco Salad
Nectarines and berries
with chocolate chip
cookies

CHICKEN TACO SALAD

1 tablespoon vegetable oil
1 pound skinless, boneless chicken breasts, cut into cubes
1 pouch CAMPBELL'S Dry Onion with Chicken Broth Soup
    and Recipe Mix
½ cup water
1 tablespoon chili powder
  Tortilla chips
8 cups salad greens torn in bite-size pieces
1 medium tomato, diced (about 1 cup)
½ cup shredded Cheddar cheese (2 ounces)
  Sour cream
  VLASIC or EARLY CALIFORNIA sliced pitted Ripe Olives

• In 10-inch skillet over medium-high heat, in hot oil, cook *half* of chicken until browned, stirring often. Remove; set aside. Repeat with remaining chicken. Pour off fat.

• Stir in soup mix, water and chili powder. Heat to boiling. Return chicken to skillet. Reduce heat to low. Cook 10 minutes or until chicken is no longer pink, stirring occasionally.

• Arrange chips and salad greens on platter. Spoon chicken mixture over lettuce and chips. Top with tomato, cheese, sour cream and olives.

Makes 4 main-dish servings

Prep Time: 15 minutes
Cook Time: 25 minutes

▼Make your own coleslaw mix from cabbage and carrots: Shred 1 small head cabbage (about 6 cups) and 2 medium carrots (about 1 cup); toss.

▼Canned tuna comes in several varieties. Solid or fancy tuna consists of large chunks. Chunk tuna has slightly smaller pieces and is great for casseroles. Flaked or grated tuna, the smallest, works best for sandwiches and is the least expensive. Quick-chill salad tip: Refrigerate the cans of tuna ahead of time.

SHORTCUT COLESLAW

1 can (10¾ ounces) CAMPBELL'S condensed Cream of Celery Soup
⅓ cup mayonnaise
⅓ cup cider vinegar
2 tablespoons sugar
1 tablespoon prepared mustard
1 teaspoon celery seed (optional)
½ teaspoon pepper
2 bags (16 ounces *each*) coleslaw mix

• In bowl, combine first 7 ingredients. Add coleslaw mix; toss to coat. Cover; chill 4 hours before serving. Garnish with *kale leaves* and *carrot curls*.

Makes about 8 cups or 16 side-dish servings

Prep Time: 10 minutes
Chill Time: 4 hours

TUNA MACARONI SALAD

1 can (10¾ ounces) CAMPBELL'S condensed Cream of Celery Soup
½ cup mayonnaise
1 small onion, finely chopped (about ¼ cup)
2 tablespoons vinegar
4 cups cooked corkscrew macaroni
2 cans (about 6 ounces *each*) tuna, drained and flaked
2 cups cooked mixed vegetables *or* peas

• In bowl, combine soup, mayonnaise, onion and vinegar; add macaroni, tuna and vegetables. Toss to coat. Cover; chill 4 hours before serving. Serve on *lettuce leaves*. Garnish with *flowering rosemary*.

Makes about 8½ cups *or* 6 main-dish servings

Prep Time: 20 minutes
Chill Time: 4 hours

Shortcut Coleslaw *(top)*
Tuna Macaroni Salad *(bottom)*

▼So you either leave them in too long or not long enough. Don't let yourself crack under the pressure of making the perfect hard-cooked egg! Put eggs in a saucepan, cover with cold water and heat to boiling over medium heat. Remove from heat. Cover; let stand for 20 minutes. Then, remove lid and run cold water over the eggs for two minutes. Always refrigerate hard-cooked eggs.

▼No time for the shell game? Buy about ½ cup hard-cooked eggs from the salad bar at your supermarket and substitute for the amount of eggs in this recipe!

CRUNCHY POTATO SALAD

9 medium potatoes, cut into 1-inch cubes (about 8½ cups)
1 can (10¾ ounces) CAMPBELL'S condensed Cream of Celery Soup
¾ cup mayonnaise
¼ cup vinegar
½ teaspoon black pepper
2 ribs celery, chopped (about 1 cup)
1 small green pepper, chopped (about ½ cup)
2 green onions, chopped (about ¼ cup)
2 hard-cooked eggs, chopped

• In 4-quart saucepan, cover potatoes with water. Over high heat, heat to boiling. Reduce heat to low. Cover; cook 15 minutes or until tender. Drain in colander.

• In large bowl, combine soup, mayonnaise, vinegar and pepper. Add potatoes, celery, green pepper, onions and eggs; toss to coat. Cover; refrigerate 6 hours before serving. If desired, serve on *lettuce;* garnish with additional *hard-cooked egg.*

Makes about 10 cups or   **Prep Time: 35 minutes**
10 side-dish servings   **Chill Time: 6 hours**

CREAMY DIJON DRESSING

1 can (10¾ ounces) CAMPBELL'S HEALTHY REQUEST
   condensed Cream of Celery Soup
½ cup reduced-calorie mayonnaise
¼ cup water
2 tablespoons vinegar
2 tablespoons Dijon-style mustard
½ teaspoon garlic powder

• In small bowl, combine soup, mayonnaise, water, vinegar, mustard and garlic powder. Cover; refrigerate 2 hours before serving. Stir before serving. Refrigerate any remaining dressing. If desired, garnish with chopped *fresh parsley.*

Makes about 2 cups   **Prep Time: 5 minutes**
                             Chill Time: 2 hours

TANGY FRENCH DRESSING

1 can (10¾ ounces) CAMPBELL'S HEALTHY REQUEST
   condensed Tomato Soup
½ cup vegetable oil
¼ cup vinegar
1 teaspoon prepared mustard

• In small bowl or jar, place soup, oil, vinegar and mustard; stir with fork or cover and shake until thoroughly mixed. Cover; refrigerate 2 hours before serving. Stir or shake dressing before serving. Refrigerate any remaining dressing. If desired, garnish with *lemon peel.*

Makes about 2 cups   **Prep Time: 5 minutes**
                             Chill Time: 2 hours

Creamy Dijon Dressing *(left)*
Tangy French Dressing *(right)*

HANDY HERB GUIDE

Use this list of common cooking herbs as a guide for seasoning foods with herbs. Before you begin, here are a few tips for using fresh and dried herbs.

▼ Because dried herbs have a stronger flavor than fresh, substitute *three times* as much of a chopped fresh herb for the dried one. For example, use 1 tablespoon chopped *fresh* dill for 1 teaspoon *dried* dill weed.

▼ After measuring dried herb leaves, crush them before using to release their aromatic oils.

▼ When using an unfamiliar herb, use about 1/4 teaspoon dried herb for 4 servings, then taste before adding more.

BASIL
▼ Fragrant leaves with a sweet spicy taste.
▼ Available: fresh or dried leaves.
▼ Use to flavor meats, poultry, soups, stews and vegetables.

BAY LEAF
▼ Green, aromatic, shiny leaves with a pungent woodsy flavor.
▼ Available: fresh or dried whole leaves. Remove leaf before serving.
▼ Use to flavor meats, soups, stews and vegetables.

CHIVES
▼ Long tubular leaves with a mild onion flavor.
▼ Available: fresh or freeze-dried.
▼ Use to flavor eggs, salads, sauces and vegetables.

CILANTRO (also known as Chinese parsley)
▼ Delicate dark green leaves with a distinctive pungent flavor.
▼ Available: fresh or dried leaves.
▼ Used in Chinese, Indian and Mexican cuisines and to flavor meats, poultry and sauces.

DILL
▼ Feathery green leaves with a delicate, distinctive flavor.
▼ Available: fresh or dried leaves (dried dill is known as dill weed) and in seeds.
▼ Use to flavor fish, pickles, poultry, salads, savory baked goods, vegetables and vinegars.

MINT
▼ The two most popular varieties are peppermint and spearmint. Peppermint has a strong, sweet cool flavor. Spearmint has a mild sweet flavor.
▼ Available: fresh or dried leaves and in extract or oil forms.
▼ Use to flavor beverages, fruits, jellies, lamb, sauces and tomatoes.

OREGANO
▼ Small green leaves with a strong, pungent, slightly bitter flavor.
▼ Available: fresh or dried leaves and ground.
▼ Use to flavor pork, lamb and vegetables.

PARSLEY
▼ Dark green leaves with a mild peppery flavor. The two most popular forms of parsley are curly leaf or flat leaf (Italian).
▼ Available: fresh or dried.
▼ Use to flavor any dish except desserts.

ROSEMARY
▼ Resembling small pine needles, the silver-green leaves are aromatic with a piny sweet flavor.
▼ Available: fresh or dried leaves.
▼ Use to flavor dressings, lamb, poultry, stuffing and vegetables.

TARRAGON
▼ Aromatic, dark green leaves with a distinctive licorice-like flavor.
▼ Available: fresh or dried leaves.
▼ Use to flavor dressings, eggs, fish, salads, sauces and vinegars.

THYME
▼ Tiny, oval-shaped, grey-green leaves with a spicy aroma and a strong, distinctive taste.
▼ Available: fresh or dried leaves and ground.
▼ Use to flavor cream sauces, fish, poultry, meat and soups.

Recipe Index

Basil Vegetable Medley, 78
Beef (*see also* Ground Beef)
    Grilled Marinated Beef, 62
    Quick Barbecued Beef
        Sandwiches, 40
    Skillet Beef Supper, 44
Bistro Onion Burgers, 60
Broccoli-Onion Dip, 8

Cajun Fish, 36
Chicken
    Chicken and Vegetables, 28
    Chicken 'n' Twists, 82
    Chicken Fajitas, 54
    Chicken in Savory Lemon Sauce, 22
    Chicken Pasta Parmesan, 30
    Chicken Taco Salad, 84
    Chunky Chicken Stir-Fry, 28
    Grilled Chicken Salad, 82
    Harvest Chicken Skillet, 16
    Herbed Brown Rice and Chicken, 20
    Herbed Chicken Kabobs, 52
    Honey-Mustard Wings, 6
    Lemony Chicken Pasta Toss, 18
    Onion Chicken Nuggets, 10
    Sassy Grilled Chicken, 52
    Sautéed Chicken Breasts, 24
Chunky Chicken Stir-Fry, 28
Cream Cheese Frosting, 12
Creamy Dijon Dressing, 90
Crunchy Potato Salad, 88

Easy Beef and Broccoli, 44

Favorite Barbecue Sauce, 66
Fish and Vegetable Skillet, 32
Fish Steaks Dijon, 58

Garlic Shrimp and Pasta, 38
Glazed Peas and Carrots, 74
Grilled Chicken Salad, 82
Grilled Marinated Beef, 62
Grilling Basics, 50-51
Ground Beef (*see also* Beef)
    Bistro Onion Burgers, 60
    Nacho Tacos, 16
    Salsa Mac 'n' Beef, 42

Ham and Pasta Skillet, 46
Handy Herb Guide, 92-93
Harvest Chicken Skillet, 16
Herb Grilling Sauce, 68
Herbed Brown Rice and Chicken, 20
Herbed Chicken Kabobs, 52
Herbed Turkey Sauté, 26
Honey-Barbecued Ribs, 64
Honey-Mustard Wings, 6

Italian Potato Topper, 72

Lemony Chicken Pasta Toss, 18

Marinated Vegetables, 78

Nacho Dip, 10
Nacho Tacos, 16
Onion Bean Bake, 76
Onion Chicken Nuggets, 10

Oriental Shrimp Kabobs, 56

Pasta
    Chicken 'n' Twists, 82
    Chicken Pasta Parmesan, 30
    Garlic Shrimp and Pasta, 38
    Ham and Pasta Skillet, 46
    Lemony Chicken Pasta Toss, 18
    Pasta Alfredo, 30
    Pasta Primavera, 72
    Potluck Vegetable Rotini, 74
    Salsa Mac 'n' Beef, 42
    Tuna Macaroni Salad, 86
Pork
    Ham and Pasta Skillet, 46
    Honey-Barbecued Ribs, 64
    Teriyaki Pork Kabobs, 66
    Sausage and Pepper Sandwiches, 46
Potato Kabobs with Cheese Sauce, 68
Potluck Vegetable Rotini, 74

Quick 'n' Easy Salmon, 34
Quick Barbecued Beef Sandwiches, 40
Quick Gazpacho, 8

Salads
    Chicken 'n' Twists, 82
    Chicken Taco Salad, 84
    Crunchy Potato Salad, 88
    Grilled Chicken Salad, 82
    Shortcut Coleslaw, 86
    Tuna Macaroni Salad, 86

RECIPE INDEX
Continued

Salad Dressings
Creamy Dijon Dressing, 90
Tangy French Dressing, 90
Salsa Mac 'n' Beef, 42

Sandwiches
Bistro Onion Burgers, 60
Nacho Tacos, 16
Quick Barbecued Beef
   Sandwiches, 40
Sausage and Pepper Sandwiches, 46
Sassy Grilled Chicken, 52

Sauces
Favorite Barbecue Sauce, 66
Herb Grilling Sauce, 68
Sausage and Pepper Sandwiches, 46
Sautéed Chicken Breasts, 24

Seafood
Cajun Fish, 36
Fish and Vegetable Skillet, 32
Fish Steaks Dijon, 58
Garlic Shrimp and Pasta, 38
Oriental Shrimp Kabobs, 56
Quick 'n' Easy Salmon, 34
Tuna Macaroni Salad, 86
Shortcut Coleslaw, 86

Side Dishes
Basil Vegetable Medley, 78
Crunchy Potato Salad, 88
Glazed Peas and Carrots, 74
Italian Potato Topper, 72
Marinated Vegetables, 78
Onion Bean Bake, 76
Pasta Primavera, 72
Potato Kabobs with Cheese Sauce, 68
Potluck Vegetable Rotini, 74
Shortcut Coleslaw, 86
Tomato-Basil Zucchini, 76
Skillet Beef Supper, 44

Skillet Dishes
Cajun Fish, 36
Chicken and Vegetables, 28
Chicken in Savory Lemon Sauce, 22
Chicken Pasta Parmesan, 30
Chunky Chicken Stir-Fry, 28
Easy Beef and Broccoli, 44
Fish and Vegetable Skillet, 32
Garlic Shrimp and Pasta, 38
Glazed Peas and Carrots, 74
Ham and Pasta Skillet, 46
Harvest Chicken Skillet, 16
Herbed Brown Rice and Chicken, 20
Herbed Turkey Sauté, 26
Lemony Chicken Pasta Toss, 18
Nacho Tacos, 16
Pasta Alfredo, 30
Quick 'n' Easy Salmon, 34
Quick Barbecued Beef
   Sandwiches, 40
Salsa Mac 'n' Beef, 42

Sausage and Pepper Sandwiches, 46
Sautéed Chicken Breasts, 24
Skillet Beef Supper, 44

Snacks
Broccoli-Onion Dip, 8
Honey-Mustard Wings, 6
Nacho Dip, 10
Onion Chicken Nuggets, 10
Quick Gazpacho, 8
Tomato Soup-Spice Cupcakes, 12
Vegetable Quesadillas, 7

Tangy French Dressing, 90
Teriyaki Pork Kabobs, 66
Tomato-Basil Zucchini, 76
Tomato Soup-Spice Cupcakes, 12
Tuna Macaroni Salad, 86

Vegetables
Basil Vegetable Medley, 78
Crunchy Potato Salad, 88
Glazed Peas and Carrots, 74
Italian Potato Topper, 72
Marinated Vegetables, 78
Onion Bean Bake, 76
Pasta Primavera, 72
Potato Kabobs with Cheese Sauce, 68
Potluck Vegetable Rotini, 74
Shortcut Coleslaw, 86
Tomato-Basil Zucchini, 76
Vegetable Quesadillas, 7

RECIPES BY PRODUCT INDEX

CAMPBELL'S CONDENSED SOUP
Broccoli Cheese Soup
  Ham and Pasta Skillet, 46

Cheddar Cheese Soup
  Chicken Fajitas, 54
  Potato Kabobs with Cheese Sauce, 68
  Salsa Mac 'n' Beef, 42
  Vegetable Quesadillas, 7

Cream of Asparagus Soup
  Basil Vegetable Medley, 78

Cream of Celery Soup
  Crunchy Potato Salad, 88
  Herbed Turkey Sauté, 26
  Shortcut Coleslaw, 86
  Tuna Macaroni Salad, 86

Cream of Chicken Soup
  Potluck Vegetable Rotini, 74

Cream of Mushroom Soup
  Italian Potato Topper, 72

Fiesta Nacho Cheese Soup
  Nacho Dip, 10
  Nacho Tacos, 16

Golden Corn Soup
  Harvest Chicken Skillet, 16

Healthy Request Ready To Serve
Chicken Broth
  Glazed Peas and Carrots, 74

Healthy Request Cream of
Broccoli Soup
  Chicken in Savory Lemon Sauce, 22

Healthy Request Cream of
Celery Soup
  Creamy Dijon Dressing, 90

Healthy Request Cream of
Mushroom Soup
  Fish and Vegetable Skillet, 32

Healthy Request Tomato Soup
  Tangy French Dressing, 90
  Tomato-Basil Zucchini, 76

Italian Tomato Soup
  Sausage and Pepper
    Sandwiches, 46
  Sautéed Chicken Breasts, 24

Tomato Soup
  Cajun Fish, 36
  Favorite Barbecue Sauce, 66
  Grilled Chicken Salad, 82
  Grilled Marinated Beef, 62
  Oriental Shrimp Kabobs, 56
  Quick Barbecued Beef Sandwiches, 40
  Quick Gazpacho, 8
  Sassy Grilled Chicken, 52
  Tomato Soup-Spice
    Cupcakes, 12

CAMPBELL'S CHUNKY SOUP
  Chicken and Vegetables, 28
  Chunky Chicken Stir-Fry, 28
  Easy Beef and Broccoli, 44

CAMPBELL'S DRY SOUP MIX
  Bistro Onion Burgers, 60
  Broccoli-Onion Dip, 8
  Chicken Taco Salad, 84
  Herbed Chicken Kabobs, 52
  Honey-Barbecued Ribs, 64
  Honey-Mustard Wings, 6

  Onion Bean Bake, 76
  Onion Chicken Nuggets, 10

CAMPBELL'S HOME COOKIN' SOUP
  Chicken Pasta Parmesan, 30
  Pasta Alfredo, 30
  Skillet Beef Supper, 44

CAMPBELL'S or SANWA RAMEN PRIDE
  Chunky Chicken Stir-Fry, 28

CAMPBELL'S PORK & BEANS
  Onion Bean Bake, 76

PACE SALSA
  Chicken Fajitas, 54
  Nacho Dip, 10
  Salsa Mac 'n' Beef, 42

PEPPERIDGE FARM
  Bistro Onion Burgers, 60

SWANSON READY TO SERVE CLEAR BROTH
  Fish Steaks Dijon, 58
  Garlic Shrimp and Pasta, 38
  Herb Grilling Sauce, 68
  Lemony Chicken Pasta Toss, 18
  Marinated Vegetables, 78
  Quick 'n' Easy Salmon, 34
  Salsa Mac 'n' Beef, 42
  Teriyaki Pork Kabobs, 66

**SWANSON NATURAL GOODNESS READY TO
SERVE CLEAR CHICKEN BROTH**
  Chicken 'n' Twists, 82
  Herbed Brown Rice and Chicken, 20
  Pasta Primavera, 72

VLASIC or EARLY CALIFORNIA OLIVES
  Chicken Taco Salad, 84